Spiritual Messages:

FROM A BOTTLE

Ann Marie Ruby

ISBN: 0692858431
ISBN-13: 978-0692858431

DEDICATION

I dedicate this book to all the souls looking for a spiritual message from a friend. Life lands us upon a journey through time. We land upon the doors of strangers, friends, and family. The tunnel continues as life is a lesson to be learned. As we cross the doors and land upon the door of a stranger, please know this stranger gives you a helping hand through my words of inspirational quotations.

I dedicate this book to all of whom need a helping hand. May there always be a helping hand for all of My Lord's creation who have ever fallen down and needed a simple lift from a stranger, your guiding Angel in disguise.

May there be an Angel in disguise at every corner of our lives. I dedicate this book to all of whom needed that inspiration, that helping hand.

Spread peace, be in peace.

INTRODUCTION

Spiritual quotations have taken birth from my inner soul. I write them from peace for peace to spread peace. I live a very simple life. Words I say are from my soul, and words carried out in anger and resentment I take them to vacation. Always after the vacation, I feel good I have not thrown out words I never shall be able to take back. In my life, words are sacred gifts from The Creator to spread with kindness. A simple compliment given I take to my soul and give it a new life in my heart, where she shall live forever. Yes, it is true, words hurt me more than I can express or ever write within words, for once it is left out, the wound never heals. Remember, where there is anger, nothing is left but ashes as anger burns all around it.

Spiritual awakening has given me the solace, the strength to walk through the blazing sun or the heavy drenched rain. I know whatever windstorms come my way, I shall take them as I know my Lord waits for me at the end of this journey. I walk on this path as a devotee of truth, just, honor, and kindness. May I be the bearer of kind words which find a space in each and all of your hearts. I write this not just as an author, but as your true friend.

I have written these simple words of inspirational quotations to be a friend when you need them and when you do not need them. They will always be there as a friend for you today and tomorrow, a friend for the future generation. Everything is lost in time, but the words remain as a gift from the past. May my words be a gift from the past to the present for the future.

MESSAGE FROM THE AUTHOR

As I had finished up my prayer book, I started writing this inspirational quotation book.

I saw a blessed dream. I was walking by a river and I had in my hands, bottles like milk bottles from the past. In each bottle, I had placed a prayer and then had them floating into the water. I had said go to where my words are needed. I asked and held them in my chest as I made them float into the water. I watched them floating away and knew my prayer book would reach those in need.

I woke up realizing there must be someone who needs the prayer book or the kind words of a friend. I have included a few prayers in this book, from my prayer book, so you can have them as a friend as well.

If I could, I would send all my prayers from my prayer book to each and all of you through a bottle in the ocean hoping it would reach the hands of my friends who but need them.

Be in peace and spread peace.

I have called this book *Spiritual Messages: From A Bottle* because of this dream.

BLESSED BE HEAVEN

My Lord, my Creator,

I search for You within the skies.

I see Your eyes watching over,

Keeping me safe from all evil eyes.

I search for You on Earth beneath,

I see my Lord holding on to me,

For it is then, I am but able to walk.

I search for You throughout the blazing desert sun,

Not fearing the burning heat.

I know the winds of my Lord cools my soul,

As the wind blows through the air,

Whispering prayers to keep me going.

I search for You in the deep blue ocean,

As I fear not the waves.

I find my Lord washing my sins away,

As I repent, repent, repent.

At the end of my day, waiting to return Home,

I realize above, around, and beyond me,

All that I see, hear, and feel,

Standing always around me,

My Lord, my Creator.

For I know I have never left Home,

For all of this is,

BLESSED BE HEAVEN.

*From my prayer book, _Spiritual Songs: Letters From My Chest_.

"*Journey* of life, I call it *time* of *reflection*, time to repent, *redeem*, *and* spiritually awaken. Leave *all the* negativities behind *and* walk *forward* with peace as our *guide*."

Quotation #1

"*Peace*,
be the teacher of *life*.
Guide me and
all of whom *seek*
you *towards* the
lane of *unity*."

Quotation #2

"*Like* a bath,
I *clean* my soul
through *peace*."

Quotation #3

"*Teachers* are the *peace* between all *differences*."

Quotation #4

"*Every* life brings the gift of *lessons* to the *doors* of the *future*."

Quotation #5

"*Past*, present, and future become *one* *through* the pages of *history*."

Quotation #6

"Peaceful encounters of *differences create* the most *beautiful rainbows."*

Quotation #7

"*Land* and water unite through *love* and break up as *anger* gets in *between*."

Quotation #8

"*Teardrops* drip from the *eyes* and have *created* the salty *ocean*."

Quotation #9

"*Sins* burden the mind and *body* weighing down the *pure soul*."

Quotation #10

"*Bridge* between life *and* death, or the past and the *future,* is the *present.*"

Quotation #11

"*Spread* love to *overcome* all obstacles *as* the *bridge* between *negativity* and *positivity* is *love*."

Quotation #12

"*Rain* pours from *Heavens* above as Mother Earth *cries* for her *children*."

Quotation #13

"*Wake* up to spread love *throughout* the *day*, for then during the dark *nights*, we shall be *safe* as we glow within *love*."

Quotation #14

"*Do* not remorse in guilt *for* it brings *you* down and all *around*."

Quotation #15

"*Be* the helping hand your *soul* seeks, for it is then *we* shall find helping *hands* all *around*."

Quotation #16

"*There* is no orphan on this *Earth* as long *as* there is a *mother* or a father *alive*."

Quotation #17

"*Hold* on to the children of this *Earth* for *they* are a *gift* from Heavens *above*."

Quotation #18

"*Earth* becomes *Heaven* through the gift of *love*."

Quotation #19

"*Mother* Earth smiles in *peace* as the *children* of Earth unite in *peace*."

Quotation #20

"*Anger* is an obstacle of *life* taking *everything* on her *way*."

Quotation #21

"*Family* is the circle
made *through* the
past, *the* present,
and the *future*."

Quotation #22

"*Each* country is
a *house* as
this *Earth* is
a *neighborhood.*"

Quotation #23

"*Each* life lies as a lesson for the *future*. As we *go* through the *pages* of known *and* unknown lives, the *lessons* are *learned*."

Quotation #24

"*Only* if we could but see *ourselves*, we would *be* our biggest *critic*."

Quotation #25

"*Religion*, race, and color *united* become a fresh *bowl* of *colorful* fruits for all *humans* and *humanity*."

Quotation #26

"*Words* travel
through *time*,
use them *wisely*."

Quotation #27

"*A* wise man and his words of *wisdom* come *after* a hard-lived *life*."

Quotation #28

"*Invisible* sins are but visible to the *soul*. Do not *hide* within them, but *burn* them with a *blessed* candle of *prayer*."

Quotation #29

"*Burn* the candles of hope for the *past*, present, and *future* to be guided *by*."

Quotation #30

"*The* lights of hope brimming *through* the eyes of a *guide* become a *torch* for all in the *dark*."

Quotation #31

"*Difference* between the told and *untold* is *the* untold *mysteries* which remain *unknown forever.*"

Quotation #32

"*Like* a newborn child, hold on to the *sweet* words. *Let* them *blossom* into nature with *love*."

Quotation #33

"*Wind* spreads harmony *from* soul to *soul*. Be the harmony. *Spread harmony*."

Quotation #34

"*Life* is but a day, so on this *day*, be an example. *For* tomorrow, *the* future shall *look* back upon the *past* and *find* you as an *example*."

Quotation #35

"*Walk* gently as you sow the *seeds*, for *tomorrow*, the plants *shall* blossom *and* be your family *tree*."

Quotation #36

"*Today*, we store all that we see *into* our *memories*. Tomorrow, *if* we get *lost*, may these memories *take* us *back* through the memory *lane*."

Quotation #37

"*Prayers* relieve the pain of one's *soul*, so *holding* on to them, *we* can finally *walk*."

Quotation #38

"*Plants* nurture us as we *nurture* them. *From* this lesson, may we be *able* to *nurture all* of whom need *care*."

Quotation #39

"*Being* a person of knowledge is *but* the *perception* of what is *known* and what *is* but *unknown*."

Quotation #40

40

"*What* is invisible is also *visible* to the *eyes* of the *beholder.*"

Quotation #41

"*Let* us the judged

not be

The *Judge*."

Quotation #42

"*Rejoice* life today, tomorrow, *and* yesterday, *for* time *takes* away *everything* but *memories.*"

Quotation #43

"*Waves* come and *break* everything, leaving behind *only* the *memories* as she rebuilds *again*."

Quotation #44

"*Sky* breaks open as lightning *strikes*. Let us take *shelter before* she burns *again*."

Quotation #45

"*Fresh* baked bread warms the *heart*. *When* placed amongst *strangers*, it *bridges* the *differences*."

Quotation #46

"*Love* each other for there is only *today*. As *tomorrow* lands upon our *door*, this day but *was*."

Quotation #47

"*Trees* watch us writing *messages* on their *chest*, leaving *behind* *memories*. As we are lost, they *share* this with the *future*."

"*If* only we could wake up the *past* to guide us through *history*."

Quotation #49

"*Concentrate* on what is but *found*, not *on* what is but *lost*."

Quotation #50

"*The* mind, body, and soul are *teachers* in *disguise*, guiding us through the *tunnel* of *knowledge*."

Quotation #51

"*Tears* are blessings from The *Lord*. As they fall, the *chest* is *unburdened*."

Quotation #52

"*Children*
become *teachers*
from the *past*
as the *future* but
lands *upon* our
doors."

Quotation #53

"*Life's* journey ends as the *traveler* is no *more*."

Quotation #54

"*Endurance* is the *journey* of the *endured*."

Quotation #55

"*Awakened,*
the *soul* is after
the *darkness*
evaporates and *dawn*
breaks *open.*"

Quotation #56

"*Time* between birth
and death *is*
also *known*
as *life*."

Quotation #57

"*Journey* in between the mind, body, *and soul* is called *the* spiritual *awakening*."

Quotation #58

"*Sweet* and sour songs of *life* *awaken* the complete *soul*."

Quotation #59

"*Love* and fear reside on the same *road*. As we *travel through*, we learn to accept *and* defeat *them*."

Quotation #60

"*Devotion* is the complete *love* of the *devoted*."

Quotation #61

"*In* school, we are until
our life *journey*
but is *complete*."

Quotation #62

"*Leaders* create the way *for* others, not *lead* themselves *through.*"

Quotation #63

"*Giving* up *everything* is not *love*. Trying to *acquire* even something *is*."

Quotation #64

"*The* first teacher and the last teacher of *life* is *oneself* as you learn to *enter* and exit, leaving *an* example for *all*."

Quotation #65

"*Kind* words left in the air *spread* far beyond as she *kisses* all throughout *time*."

Quotation #66

"*Words* shot out of *anger* become enemies of *time*."

Quotation #67

"*Become* an obstacle for *all* anger, war, *and* resentment for then, we shall *have* the *clearance* for *peace*."

Quotation #68

68

"*Peace* knocks on the *door* as we *give* up anger, resentment, and *war*."

Quotation #69

"*Honor* and justice knock on our *door* as we become the *just* and *honorable*."

Quotation #70

"*Travel* through time, through *kindness*. *For* even when all is lost, *kindness* is but *found*."

Quotation #71

"*The* ocean, the land, and the *skies* are all *witnesses* of the past, *present*, and the *future*."

Quotation #72

"*The* ark carries all life *throughout* the *storms*, if only we can *make* it *aboard*."

Quotation #73

"*The* lighthouse lights throughout the *dark* nights for all *lost souls* to be found. *May* we not fall *asleep* and miss her call of *warning.*"

Quotation #74

"*When* life gets lost and *lonely*, accept the *complete* *stranger* who finds you as a *friend.*"

Quotation #75

"*Do* not hide
in a *tunnel* for then
you *shall* be
lost."

Quotation #76

"*Forever*
there is *love* amongst
strangers who
wait for a *friend*."

Quotation #77

"*Be* the friend
you *ask* of to be
there for *you*."

Quotation #78

"*Follow* the light throughout *history* for it shall *guide* you *out* of the dark into the *light*."

Quotation #79

"*Difference* between the *daylight* and the darkness *is* *knowledge* to see the *difference.*"

Quotation #80

"*When* nightmare knocks *upon* our *door*, remember with *time*, we shall but wake up from *it*."

Quotation #81

"*Dreams* are a form of *blessings* from the *unknown.*"

Quotation #82

"*Even* though it seems like *your destiny* is frozen *and* nothing is *happening*, time shall *pass* by and *you* shall be *at* your *destination*."

Quotation #83

"*Peace* is achieved *every* day through give and *take*."

Quotation #84

"*Life* stays still as *everything* else *moves* on. What is *found* is not needed *until* it too is but *gone*."

"*Give* and take is a *perception* of the mind. *Soul* gives *all* and takes *nothing.*"

Quotation #86

"*Eternal* truth of life is eternal *love*, only found in *eternity*."

Quotation #87

"*My* house is a shelter for all *miracles* of life which *include* the *non-believers* and the *believers*."

Quotation #88

"*Shelter* I find *amongst* the *strangers* whom but are *Angels* in *disguise.*"

Quotation #89

"*Standing* up against a *stranger* is but easy. The *hard* part is *standing* up against your *own* who but is *wrong*."

Quotation #90

"*Listen* to all. Give an ear to the *stranger* too, for *remember* the *Angel* your eyes are *searching* for *may* be a total *stranger* in *disguise*."

Quotation #91

"*The* goal of life is not the *achievements*, but the *journey* through *it*."

Quotation #92

"*Do* not give up on
hope for remember
hope is *but*
immortal."

Quotation #93

"*Love* is always *waiting* for us at the *door* for even though *all* but fade *away*, love is *steadfast* as she is *immortal*."

Quotation #94

"*Trials* of life get us *ready* for the final Judgment *Day*."

Quotation #95

"*Day* breaks open through *the* darkness. Remember *this* as *you* are but *lost within* the *darkness*."

Quotation #96

"*Inspiration* is but the *gift* of an inspired *soul*."

Quotation #97

"*Live* life to inspire others to *follow* the inspiration of *life*."

Quotation #98

"*Achievements*
arrive at the *door*
of the *achiever* as
the journey is *made*."

Quotation #99

"*Mercy* is but found at the *door* of the *merciful.*"

Quotation #100

"*Time* passes by us.
Words stay forever
as a *guide* and
become a guide for
the *future*."

Quotation #101

"*Life* is a blessed
spiritual *journey*."

Quotation #102

"*Love* withstands time. Time *leaves* us as she *crosses* our door. *Love* leaves us with sweet *and* sour *memories*, *keeping* time alive *forever*."

Quotation #103

"*May* we be a helping *hand* to all as we cross *and* learn *from* our own *battles*."

Quotation #104

"*Spiritual*
connection *between*
all *humans*
is the inner *soul*."

Quotation #105

"*Love* is a one-way journey from *birth* to *death*."

Quotation #106

"*May* my words
be a *friend*, an
inspiration. May
they *catch* your
teardrops, *and* remind
you there is always
tomorrow."

Quotation #107

"*Life* is a spiritual *journey* where we *battle* negativity with *positivity*."

Quotation #108

"*The* war between negativity *and* positivity is *won through* the battles of *life*."

Quotation #109

"*Come* and join me on this journey of giving and maybe together, we can be the hope, the motivation, the inspiration for a stranger waiting for a knock on the door from a stranger who I call my Angel in *disguise*."

"*The* difference between *an* Angel and demon is the *will* to do *good* from the inner *soul*."

Quotation #111

"*My* life is a journey through *struggles* and *achievements* of *life*. Throughout *all*, it was a test as to see if I *could* *withstand* the winds *of* obstacles and hold *on*."

Quotation #112

"*Words* give me the power to *withstand* all *obstacles*, *even* though they hurt, I *learned* to take the *bite* and hold the tears *back*."

Quotation #113

"*It* is the *tears* who *gave* me out to so many even *though* I had *warned* her to please remain *quiet*."

Quotation #114

"*How* do we cross
the bridge of pain?
Physical pain,
take a painkiller, but
the other one?
I knew words
were powerful
as on my journey,
I had seen the
best therapy was
kindness and
words."

Quotation #115

"*Prayers* are blessed words, and *poems* are *sweet* words, so I had taken the *help* from this *powerful* friend *who* is known as *word*."

Quotation #116

"*Words* hurt as they are *thrown* out as a curse, or bring *joy* and *harmony* as they are *given* as a *poem* or a sweet *song*."

Quotation #117

"*I* was able to cross the *bridge* of *courage*, fear, *anger*, resentment, *and* all the obstacles that life *brings* forth to *us*."

Quotation #118

"*Dedication* is *given* as an *admiration* of the *admired*."

Quotation #119

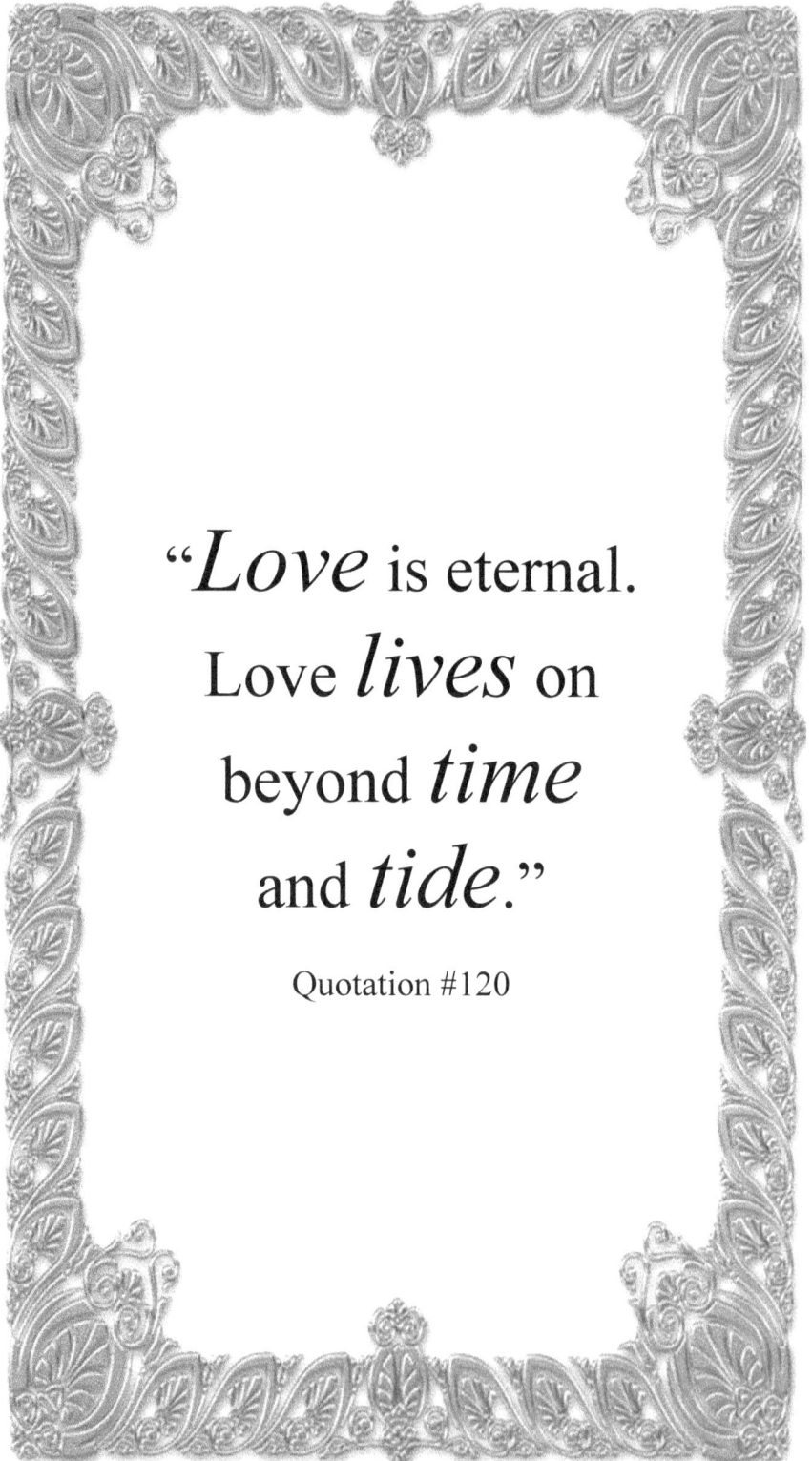

"*Love* is eternal.
Love *lives* on
beyond *time*
and *tide*."

Quotation #120

"*Love* learns to swim
across the *ocean*
to *unite* with
the *beloved*."

Quotation #121

"*Hope* withstands the *struggles* of life as she sees past *time* and *tide*."

Quotation #122

"*Time* is held to stay still in the *frames* of the *eyes* of the *beholder.*"

Quotation #123

"*The* soul remains *forever* within the *heart* of the true *beloved*."

Quotation #124

"*From* soul to *soul*, the beloved *belongs*."

Quotation #125

"*Love's* true victory
is the *heart* of the
beholder."

Quotation #126

"*Children* are the *soul* of this *universe*. Within their *journey*, life is but *complete*."

Quotation #127

"*Children* say what is but *lost* to all, the *complete innocence* of the *universe*, the *truth*."

Quotation #128

"*Complete* truth is found *within* the *awakening* spirit of the *creation.*"

Quotation #129

"*All* creation are but the complete *love* of The *Creator.*"

Quotation #130

"*Spiritual awakening* helps the *soul* to forgive *everything*, the *humans*, the *animals*, the *obstacles* of life, as we *grow* from *within*."

Quotation #131

"*Forgiveness* rejuvenates *the* inner soul as *love* removes all the *obstacles.*"

Quotation #132

"*Life's* biggest *enemies* come from within one's *self*, as we *carry* anger, resentment, *and* jealousy within *us*."

Quotation #133

"*Let* go of all the anger and *resentment*, and feel the soul *glow* from *within*."

Quotation #134

"*My* life's journey *shall* include *removing* obstacles *from* the path as the *travelers* behind *me* shall then find a *road* created *without* the burden called *obstacles*."

Quotation #135

"*May* I be the *unknown* face who inspires *you* *throughout* time, for if my *face* is *known* to you, I *then* become just another *name*."

Quotation #136

"*Mind*, body, and soul *awaken* as we *cleanse* the burden from *within*."

Quotation #137

"*No* failure in life is a *failure*, for as you fail, you *teach* others what to *avoid*."

Quotation #138

"*Life* is a blessing. Love life *for* when life is *no* more, love *carries* life through *eternity*."

Quotation #139

"*Love* is all about *giving* and the feeling to give more, *for* with the *gift* of giving, *love* becomes *eternal*."

Quotation #140

"*Mother* Earth *embraces* all of her *children* under one *blanket* as we *sleep* on our Earthly *bed*."

Quotation #141

"*The* shelter,
the *food*, and the
sustenance,
all are *given* to me by
my Mother *Earth*."

Quotation #142

"*Soul* searching helps mend all *emotional* problems. *Only* step to it is *finding* oneself *first*."

Quotation #143

"*Do* not get lost amidst *the* obstacles *of* the *world*. Find yourself *as* you get rid *of* all the obstacles *from* this *world*."

Quotation #144

144

"*The* wind
and *the* windchimes,
singing the songs
of *love*, trying
to *unite* the world,
they send this
music through all
the open *windows*."

Quotation #145

"*Time* is not a friend as he *passes* us by. *Take* this moment, *catch* him through your *memories* forever. So *even* after his *departure*, memories *frame* him *forever*."

Quotation #146

"*Yearning* for *the* sweet *memories* of *yesteryears*, go *back* in time *through* the memory *lane*."

Quotation #147

"*Arts* framed
on the *wall* are but
material.
Memories framed
in the *heart* become
immortal."

Quotation #148

"*Become* the lantern for all *humanity* as your *words* carried by *mouth* to mouth is the *oil* that shall *keep* this lantern *going* throughout *eternity*."

Quotation #149

"*Children* are the candles of *hope* guiding *all* throughout *eternity*, for they *have* been passing the candles *on*."

Quotation #150

"*The* lighthouse,
the sea, the *boat* all
have the *journey*
of the traveler *within*
their *memories*."

Quotation #151

"*Peace* breezing through the *air*, as the *windmills* and *windchimes* spread this *message* to each and all *hearts* searching for *her*."

Quotation #152

"*Land,*
water, and sea all
are but within the
dreams of the dreamers.
Open your eyes
and let all
of these dreams
become reality as you
take your step through
land, water, and

sea."

Quotation #153

ABOUT THE AUTHOR

I am an unknown person who lived the struggles, overcame the obstacles, as I have endured the pain and joy of life as they landed upon my door.

I like to be the unknown face to whom all can relate. I want you to see your face in the mirror when you search for me, not mine. For if it is my face in the mirror, then my friend you see a stranger. The unknown face is there so you see only yourself, your struggles, your achievements as you cross the journey of life. I want to be the face of a white, black, and brown, as well as the love we are always searching eternally for. If this world would have allowed, I would have distributed this inspirational quotation book to you with my own hands as a gift from a friend. Please take this book as a message from a friend.

You have my name and know I will always be there for anyone who seeks me. You can follow me @AnnahMariahRuby on Twitter, Ann Marie on my personal Facebook profile where the username is /annah.mariah.735, @TheAnnMarieRuby on my Facebook page, ann_marie_ruby on Instagram, and @TheAnnMarieRuby on Pinterest.

For more information about any one of my books, please visit my website www.annmarieruby.com.

I have published four books of original inspirational quotations:

Spiritual Travelers: Life's Journey From The Past To The Present For The Future

154

Spiritual Messages: From A Bottle

Spiritual Journey: Life's Eternal Blessings

Spiritual Inspirations: Sacred Words Of Wisdom

For all of you whom have requested my complete inspirational quotations, now I have for all of you, my complete ark of inspiration, I but call:

Spiritual Ark: The Enchanted Journey Of Timeless Quotations.

I have also published a book of original prayers:

Spiritual Songs: Letters From My Chest.

I am blessed to also share with you information about my upcoming book:

Spiritual Lighthouse: The Dream Diaries Of Ann Marie Ruby.

I give a sample from my prayer book, *Spiritual Songs: Letters From My Chest* as I have written this book of prayers from my heart for all of whom seek the spiritual journey.

GLORY BE TO MY LORD

My Lord, as dawn breaks open

Through the night sky,

May I, Your devotee, only worship You.

My Lord, with this first sight of light,

May I, Your devotee, only worship You.

My Lord, after the dark night's struggle,

The sparkling array of the morning light

Glorifies the Earth.

On this day, may I, Your devotee,

Only worship You.

My Lord, as the sun reaches through

To each and all of Your creation,

May we, the creation, say in union,

"GLORY BE TO MY LORD."

*From my prayer book, *Spiritual Songs: Letters From My Chest*.

My Spiritual Collection

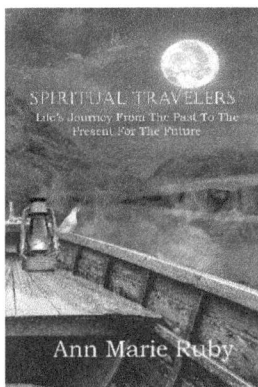

Spiritual Travelers:
Life's Journey From
The Past To The Present
For The Future

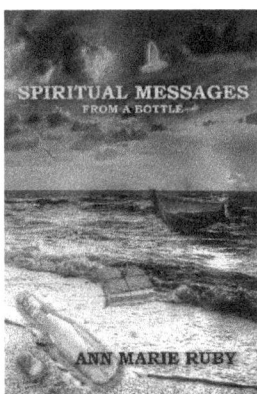

Spiritual Messages:
From A Bottle

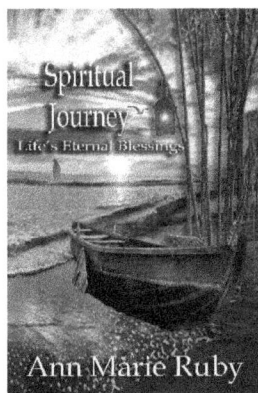

Spiritual Journey:
Life's Eternal Blessings

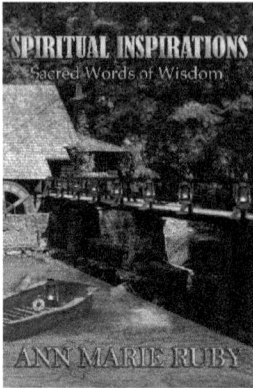

Spiritual Inspirations:
Sacred Words Of
Wisdom

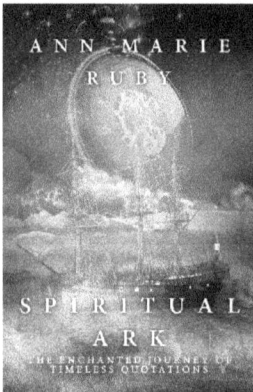

Spiritual Ark:
The Enchanted
Journey Of Timeless
Quotations

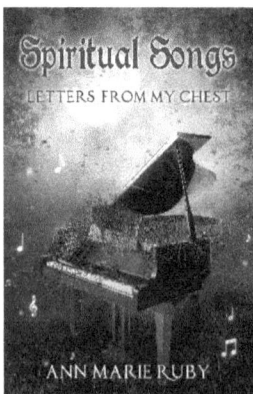

Spiritual Songs:
Letters From My Chest

158

My Upcoming Book

Spiritual Lighthouse:
The Dream Diaries Of Ann Marie Ruby

Within the dark, starless, foggy nights, my dreams appeared like the lighthouse always guiding me throughout my life. Dreams are spiritual guidance from the unknown. When the human body but falls asleep, it is then that our spiritual soul guides us throughout eternity. The soul walks into a parallel world where the past and the future exist in the same universe. Walk with me, as my soul but has walked the past and the future all throughout my life. Warnings, dangers, and surprises came upon my door, always guiding me like a lighthouse blinking in the dark night's sky. Alone, lost, and stranded I was until a lighthouse appeared within the ocean of the lost, my blessed dreams.

Take my hands and walk with me along this very personal path, as we journey together through my dream diaries, I call her, *Spiritual Lighthouse: The Dream Diaries Of Ann Marie Ruby*.

"Dreams are given from the Heavens above onto all within the Earth beneath for within them lie the miracles of eternity.

www.ingramcontent.com/pod-product-compliance
Lightning Source LLC
Chambersburg PA
CBHW031959040426
42448CB00006B/428